# LEGACIES

## *from*

# ANCIENT EGYPT

**Anita Ganeri**

Belitha Press

First published in the UK in 1999 by
Belitha Press Limited, London House,
Great Eastern Wharf, Parkgate Road,
London SW11 4NQ

ISBN 1 84138 064 4

British Library Cataloguing in Publication Data for
this book is available from the British Library.

Printed in China

Editor: Veronica Ross
Designer: Rosamund Saunders
Picture Researcher: Diana Morris
Consultant: Sallie Purkis
Illustrator: Jackie Harland

## PHOTO CREDITS
AKG London: 22cr; f cover b, 2br, 11cr, 14b, 18cr, 20, 24br, 26br
Erich Lessing. Bridgeman Art Library: 21tr. Bridgeman Art
Library/Giraudon: 7bl, 23bl. British Museum: 5bl ET Archive;
7tr, 18br, 29tl Werner Forman Archive. Cheops Barque Museum:
13bl Werner Forman Archive. James Davis Travel Photography:
21br. C.M.Dixon: f cover inset, 6bl, 15cl, 17cr, 22bl, 26bl, 27c, 28.
Egyptian Museum, Cairo: 2, 29c Bridgeman Art Library
/Giraudon; 15cr AKG London; 21c, 23cr Werner Forman Archive.
El-Minya Mus, Egypt: 18c Werner Forman Archive. Eye
Ubiquitous:12bl Steve Lindridge; 4b Mike Southern; f cover t, 10t,
11bl, 13t Julia Waterlow. Werner Forman Archive: 27t. Hutchison
Picture Library: 16cl; 8bl,9cr Jeremy Horner; 11br Chris Parker;
5br Micha Scorer. Jurgen Liepe Photo-Archiv: b cover, 5cl, 14l,
16b, 24bl, 29b. The Louvre: 25tr ET Archive. National Museum
of Archaeology, Naples: 4cl AKG London. Photostage: 9br
Donald Cooper. Powerstock/Zefa: 6tr, 18bl Simon Heaton; 17bl
Hoa-Qui; 1, 3, 8cr Brad Walker.

THE DATES IN THIS BOOK
BC (Before Christ) is used with dates of events that
happened before the birth of Christ. AD (Anno Domini,
from the Latin for 'in the year of our Lord') is used with
dates of events that happened after the birth of Christ.
The letter c used in the text stands for the Latin word
circa, and means about.

Some of the more unfamiliar words used in this book
are explained in the glossary on page 30.

# CONTENTS

# INTRODUCTION

A legacy is something handed down from one person or generation to another. It may be an object, a lifestyle, or a way of thinking or doing things. The Ancient Egyptians lived four thousand years ago, but the legacy of their brilliant culture still lives on today. The Ancient Egyptians were among the first people to use a 365-day calendar, and systems of numbers and writing. They built huge monuments, many of which still stand. These include the pyramids, built as tombs for the Egyptian kings, and spectacular reminders of Ancient Egypt's past.

## FAMOUS PEOPLE

The Greek historian, Herodotus (c 484-420 BC), made a grand tour of Ancient Egypt. He wrote a book about his travels, called the *Histories*. In it he described many aspects of Ancient Egyptian culture, including mummification. He wrote that Egypt had 'wonders more in number than those of any other land and works to show beyond expression great'.

*In his* Histories, *Herodotus described many of the sights and sounds of Ancient Egypt.*

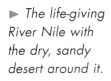 ▶ *The life-giving River Nile with the dry, sandy desert around it.*

Parent focus

## Who were the Ancient Egyptians?

The Ancient Egyptians were the people who lived in Egypt from about 3000 BC to 30 BC. During this time, they built one of the world's oldest and greatest civilizations. It was also one of the longest lasting, thriving for over 2000 years.

For most of its history, Ancient Egypt was ruled by kings called pharaohs. The Egyptians believed that the king was the god, Horus, in human form. This made him very powerful.

## The land of Egypt

Ancient Egypt was a long, narrow country stretching along the banks of the River Nile. To the east and west lay dry, dusty desert where little could live or grow. The Egyptians thought that the desert was a dangerous place. They called it Deshret, or Red Land. Most people lived in the Nile River valley. Each year, the river flooded, depositing rich, black soil, which was ideal for farming. This was called Kemet, or Black Land.

## How do we know?

We know a great deal about Ancient Egypt from the ruins and artefacts left behind. Many stone buildings and monuments have survived, preserved in the hot, dry climate. The Egyptians were buried with personal possessions such as jewellery, furniture, food and drink. They decorated their tomb walls with paintings of the gods and everyday life. Together with ancient texts and inscriptions, these have helped us to build up a vivid picture of Egyptian times.

The Cairo Museum where many Egyptian treasures are on show.

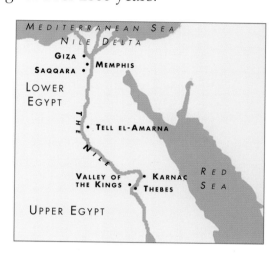

▲ This map shows Ancient Egypt and its position along the banks of the River Nile.

▲ A wall painting from an Ancient Egyptian tomb showing a shop selling geese or chickens.

# KEY DATES IN

**5000 BC**     **3000 BC**     **2000 BC**

**c 5000-3100 BC** The Predynastic Period. Several different settlements develop along the River Nile. These gradually form two kingdoms – Lower Egypt in the Nile Delta and Upper Egypt in the Nile River valley.

**c 4000 BC** Boats with sails are used on the Nile.

**c 3200 BC** A form of writing called hieroglyphics is used in Egypt for the first time.

**c 3100 BC** King Narmer (or Menes) unites Upper and Lower Egypt. He builds his capital at Memphis. He establishes the first Egyptian dynasty, known as Dynasty 1.

**c 3100-2686 BC** The Archaic Period – 1st to 2nd dynasties.

**c 2686-2181 BC** The Old Kingdom – 3rd to 6th dynasties. A time of expansion, culture and scholarship. This was also the great age of pyramid building.

**c 2589-2566 BC** Reign of King Khufu (Cheops) of the 4th dynasty. The Great Pyramid is built at Giza as a tomb for King Khufu. The Sphinx is also built.

**c 2494-2345 BC** The kings of the 5th dynasty devote themselves to the sun god, Ra, and take the title Son of Ra.

**c 2246-2150 BC** The reign of King Pepy II of the 6th dynasty. This is the longest reign of any monarch in history.

**c 2181-2040 BC** The First Intermediate Period – 7th to 10th dynasties.

**c 2040-1640 BC** The Middle Kingdom – 11th to 13th dynasties. King Mentuhotep II of the 11th dynasty reunites Egypt and restores order, which had broken down with the death of Pepy II. He makes his capital at Thebes.

# ANCIENT EGYPT

**1550 BC**          **1000 BC**          **30 BC**

**c 1640-1552 BC** The Second Intermediate Period – 14th to 17th dynasties. A period of decline.

**c 1085-664 BC** The Third Intermediate Period – 21st to 25th dynasties. Royal power declines and the empire begins to break down.

**c 1290-1224 BC** Reign of King Ramesses II (19th dynasty). He builds many great temples including Abu Simbel.

**c 1552-1085 BC** The New Kingdom – 18th to 20th dynasties. King Ahmose (18th dynasty) drives the Hyksos out. Egypt goes on to build a huge empire and become the greatest power in the Middle East. Royal tombs are built in the Valley of the Kings.

**c 664-332 BC** The Late Period – 26th to 30th dynasties.

**c 1479-1425 BC** Reign of King Tuthmosis III (18th dynasty). Egypt is at the peak of its power and influence.

**c 525-404 BC** The Persians invade Egypt and rule as the 27th dynasty.

**c 1364-1347 BC** Reign of King Akhenaten (18th dynasty). He makes major changes to Egyptian religion, introducing the worship of Aten, the sun god, and banning the worship of the old gods and goddesses. He builds a new capital at modern day Tell el-Amarna.

**332 BC** Alexander the Great takes control of Egypt. He founds the city of Alexandria which becomes a great centre of learning and culture. Great scholars come from all over the world to study at its university.

**323-30 BC** After Alexander's death, Egypt is ruled by the Ptolemies.

**c 1347-1337 BC** Reign of King Tutankhamun (18th dynasty). He is buried in the Valley of the Kings.

**30 BC** Queen Cleopatra, the last of the Ptolemaic rulers, is defeated by the Romans and commits suicide. Egypt becomes a province of the Roman Empire.

# THE STORY OF EGYPT

The earliest settlements in Ancient Egypt were farming villages which grew up about 7000 years ago. In time, these villages became part of two kingdoms – Upper Egypt in the Nile River valley and Lower Egypt in the Nile Delta. In about 3100 BC, King Narmer (or Menes) of Upper Egypt conquered Lower Egypt and united the two kingdoms. He became the first king of the first dynasty, one of the 31 Egyptian dynasties.

## IMPACT

The Greeks (under Alexander the Great), and later, the Romans, were impressed and inspired by Egyptian religion, learning and art. Much of our information about Ancient Egypt comes from their written records. Ancient Egyptian influence has lasted right into the twentieth century. The Art Deco movement of the 1920s/30s used the strong lines and geometric shapes favoured by the Ancient Egyptians.

*A hotel in Miami, Florida, USA, built in the Art Deco style.*

◄ *The Sphinx and the Great Pyramid at Giza, the most famous legacies of Ancient Egypt.*

## The Old Kingdom

One of the greatest periods in Egypt's long history began in the third dynasty during the time of the Old Kingdom. A strong central government ruled the country and Egypt grew wealthy on trade. Egyptian art, culture and scholarship flourished. This was also the great age of pyramid building (see pages 16-19). Many texts and objects from tombs survive from this time.

## The Middle Kingdom

A period of civil war followed the collapse of the Old Kingdom. Then in about 1991 BC, a high-ranking official called Amenemhat seized the throne and founded the twelfth dynasty. Amenemhat and his successors helped make Egypt strong again. But a series of weak kings led the next few dynasties. By about 1670 BC, the Hyksos people from Asia had overrun Egypt and seized control.

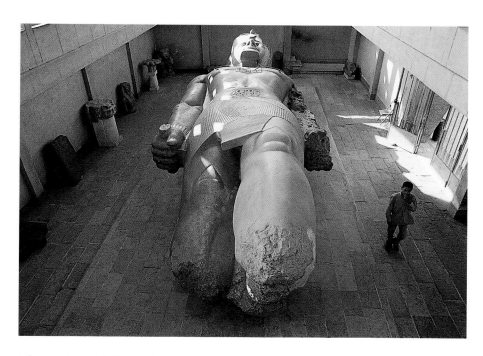

◄ A huge statue of Ramesses II of the nineteenth dynasty, one of the greatest Ancient Egyptian kings.

## The New Kingdom

The New Kingdom, which began in about 1552 BC, was a glorious period for Egypt. The Hyksos were driven out and Egyptian forces, led by King Ahmose, conquered a vast empire. Under King Tuthmosis III, Egypt reached the height of its powers. During the reign of Ramesses III, Egypt was attacked by the Sea Peoples. Despite an Egyptian victory, the country began slowly to decline. After the twentieth dynasty, it was ruled by a series of foreign kings. In 332 BC, Egypt was conquered by Alexander the Great. In 30 BC, it became a province of the Roman Empire.

### FAMOUS PEOPLE

After Alexander's death, his general Ptolemy ruled Egypt. He began the Ptolemaic Dynasty. The last and most famous Ptolemy was Queen Cleopatra (ruled 51-30 BC). She married the Roman ruler Mark Antony. Defeated by the rival Roman army of Octavian (later the emperor Augustus), Antony and Cleopatra committed suicide. Their tragic love story has inspired many writers and poets, including William Shakespeare.

A modern performance of Antony and Cleopatra.

# GIFT OF THE NILE

The Greek writer Herodotus called Egypt the 'gift of the Nile'. The River Nile flows north from central Africa through Egypt to its delta in the Mediterranean Sea. Then, as now, it was vital to Egypt's wealth and well-being. Each year the river flooded and deposited rich, black mud along its banks. This created fertile farmland in an area that would otherwise have been parched desert, and allowed farmers to grow huge supplies of crops. The river was also Egypt's main highway and its main source of water for drinking and irrigation.

▲ *Water from the River Nile still irrigates farmers' fields as it did in ancient times.*

## FAMOUS PEOPLE

The Ancient Egyptians believed that the flooding of the Nile was controlled by the god, Hapi. He was often shown dressed as a fisherman with a headdress made of water plants. He carried a tray of food in his hands, symbolizing the riches provided by the life-giving Nile.

## The farming year

The farming year was divided into three seasons. In July, the river began to flood. This was called the Inundation. While their fields lay underwater, many farmers went to work for the king on building projects. When the floods went down in November, the farmers sowed their seed. This was the growing season. The harvest was in March and April.

## Crops and food

Agriculture was the mainstay of the Egyptian economy. Most farmers worked on the estates of wealthy landowners, paying rent for their fields in crops. The main crops were wheat and barley, which were used to make bread and beer. Farmers also grew vegetables, fruit, including grapes for wine-making, and flax for making linen for clothes.

▶ *A tomb painting of famers hard at work with the harvest.*

### IMPACT

Since the building of the Aswan High Dam in the 1960s, the River Nile no longer floods as it did in ancient times. Water for irrigation and hydroelectric power is now stored behind the dam in Lake Nasser. This means that modern farmers have water for their fields all year round. They do not have the anxious wait of their ancient ancestors. Then, if the flood did not come, famine followed.

*The Aswan High Dam stops the River Nile from flooding.*

## Water management

Irrigation was essential in Ancient Egypt because the weather was so hot and dry. When the floods went down, farmers built ditches and canals to bring water from the Nile to their fields. The ditches and canals were also used to store water. To raise water up from the river, farmers used a device called a shaduf. It is still sometimes used in Egypt today.

▼ *Using a shaduf to raise water from the river to the fields.*

# SHIPS AND SAILS

Apart from being a major source of water, the River Nile was also the main transport route in Ancient Egypt. It is still important today. Every day, the river was crowded with rafts, boats and barges. They carried goods, passengers and huge stones for building. Funeral barges took the bodies of royal or wealthy Egyptians to their tombs. The earliest Egyptian boats were made from the papyrus reeds that grew along the river. They were pushed along with poles or oars.

## IMPACT

The modern Suez Canal links the Mediterranean Sea and the Red Sea, cutting thousands of kilometres off the sea route from northern Europe to Asia. It was completed in 1869. But the idea is much older than that. The first Suez Canal was begun by the Egyptians some 2500 years earlier in about 600 BC. It was completed by the Persians about a hundred years later and used for over a thousand years before being filled in.

*Ships and tugs on the modern Suez Canal.*

► *Barges carried the bodies of wealthy Egyptians down the river to their tombs.*

## Sailing ships

The Ancient Egyptians made many important contributions to the history of water transport. By about 3200 BC, they had invented sails. Because the wind in Egypt usually blows from north to south, the Egyptians worked out that sails would harness the power of the wind for journeys up the Nile. We know this from a picture found on an Egyptian pot. About 200 years later, shipbuilders started to build ships with wooden planks instead of reeds.

▲ Sailing ships called feluccas are a common sight on the Nile today, as they were in ancient times.

## The Egyptian navy

When the Sea Peoples from the north-east Mediterranean invaded Egypt, Ramesses III (ruled 1184-1153 BC) sent a fleet of warships against them. This was one of the first organized navies in the ancient world. It defeated the Sea Peoples in a famous battle at the mouth of the River Nile. One of the reasons for the Egyptians' success was that their warships had both oars and sails. This made them more manoeuvrable. The Sea People's ships had only sails.

◄ King Khufu's boat, pieced back together again.

### FAMOUS PEOPLE

Queen Hatshepsut ruled Egypt from 1473-1458 BC. One of her greatest achievements was to send an expedition to the land of Punt, thought to lie on the east coast of Africa. Its task was to bring back incense. Such an ambitious expedition had never been tried before and a fleet of five ships was specially built for the voyage. It was a great success.

## Boats to heaven

The Ancient Egyptians believed that after death, the soul of the king was carried by boat to the next world. In 1952, archaeologists made an extraordinary find. Buried in a pit next to the Great Pyramid at Giza, they found an almost perfectly preserved wooden ship. It lay dismantled into 1224 pieces. When it was reconstructed, it formed a boat over 20 metres long and 6 metres wide. It had been built for King Khufu 4500 years ago. It is now on display in its own museum next to the Great Pyramid.

# LIFE AFTER DEATH

T he Ancient Egyptians believed in life after death. When you died, your soul travelled to an underworld called Duat. To enjoy eternal life in the next world, though, you also needed your body. This is why the Egyptians went to such great lengths to make sure that bodies were preserved for the afterlife and not left to rot away. They achieved this using a process called mummification.

◀ *King Tutankhamun's solid gold coffin.*

▲ *The coffin was touched with magical instruments so that the mummy could speak, see and hear in the next world.*

## Making a mummy

When a body was mummified, the brain and other organs were removed and stored in special jars. Only the heart was left. Then the body was packed in natron salt to dry it out. Next it was padded with cloth or sawdust, oiled and wrapped in bandages. Lucky charms were tucked between the layers and the mummy was placed inside a coffin. This process took two months to complete.

## The Feather of Truth

It was believed that when your soul reached Duat, it had to pass a series of tests before it reached the heavenly Kingdom of the West. In the Judgement Hall of Osiris, god of the dead, your heart was weighed against the Feather of Truth. A wicked heart would tip the scales and be fed to a monster. A good heart would weigh the same as the feather, and you could continue on your journey.

▼ *The ceremony of the weighing of the heart against the Feather of Truth.*

### IMPACT

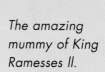

Mummification worked so well that many bodies have survived, remarkably intact. One of the most famous was the mummy of Ramesses II, discovered and unwrapped in 1881. Using X-rays and scanners to examine mummies, modern archaeologists have been able to tell what food the Egyptians ate, what illnesses they suffered and what sort of work they did.

*The amazing mummy of King Ramesses II.*

### FAMOUS PEOPLE

Anubis, the son of Osiris, was the god of mummification. He was often shown with a jackal's head. It was black because this was the colour of the rich mud deposited by the river, and therefore of life itself. The priest who led the funeral ceremony wore the jackal mask of Anubis as he performed his work.

## Guides to the afterlife

The Ancient Eygptians believed that the next life would be much like this one, only better. They filled their tombs with objects they might need. These included furniture, jewellery, clothes, food, and even models of servants to do all the work. They also had prayers and spells carved on to the tomb walls or written on scrolls of papyrus. These were like guide-books to the next world. Many of these texts have been found and studied.

# MIGHTY MONUMENTS

### FAMOUS PEOPLE

The very first pyramid was built in about 2600 BC at Saqqara as a tomb for King Djoser. It had stepped rather than slanting sides. It was designed by the royal architect, Imhotep. A brilliant scholar and statesman, he was also a doctor and high priest and may have helped to invent the calendar. After his death, he was worshipped as a god.

*King Djoser's stepped pyramid as it looks today.*

One of the greatest legacies of Ancient Egypt are the tombs built for the pharaohs. The most famous of these are the pyramids. The world's oldest and largest stone structures, these mighty monuments were so cleverly constructed that they still survive four thousand years after they were built. Their sloping sides were said to be gigantic staircases for the dead king's soul to climb to join the sun god.

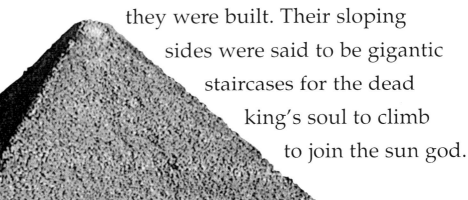

◀ *The magnificent Great Pyramid at Giza.*

## Great Pyramid

The largest pyramid was the Great Pyramid at Giza, near Cairo, one of the Seven Wonders of the World. Built for King Khufu in about 2566 BC, it stands about 140 metres high. This huge monument contains over 2 million limestone blocks, weighing from 2.5 to 15 tonnes each. It probably took about 20 years to complete. Two other pyramids stand nearby, built for kings Khafre and Menkaure.

## Building a pyramid

Building a pyramid was very hard work. First the labourers had to drag the huge stones into place on wooden sledges, up a spiralling series of mud ramps. The pyramid gradually grew higher, layer by layer, until finally the capstone was added and the whole pyramid covered with brilliant white limestone blocks. These have since been stripped away or stolen.

### IMPACT

In 1989, a glass pyramid was built over the entrance to the Louvre Museum in Paris. One of the world's most famous art galleries, the Louvre houses many priceless works of art, including the Mona Lisa by Leonardo da Vinci. Many people objected to the pyramid, saying that it was too modern!

The Louvre pyramid in Paris.

▲ This painting shows the king's body being taken down the river to his tomb.

## The final journey

The king's body was brought to the pyramid in a highly decorated funeral barge. It was prepared for burial in the riverbank temple, then carried up a causeway to the mortuary temple for prayers. Then the body was taken to the burial chamber, deep inside the pyramid, among the maze of corridors, passageways, air shafts and galleries.

# EGYPTIAN BUILDERS

The pyramids were remarkable feats of engineering. The Egyptians had no cranes, trucks or other machinery to make their lives easier. Yet they managed to build some of the greatest stone monuments ever seen. The work was done by thousands of labourers, using simple tools, ropes, ramps and sledges. At first the workers were mostly farmers, drafted in to work for the king as part of the labour tax they owed him. Later, prisoners of war were also used.

▲ This picture of Egyptian stonemasons at work was carved on to stone.

### FAMOUS PEOPLE

During Queen Hatshepsut's reign (1473-1458 BC), a man called Senmut rose from humble beginnings to become the Royal Architect and Minister of Public Works. He was in charge of building the queen's magnificent temple at Deir el Bahari, much of which can still be seen today.

## Tools and materials

The main building stones in Ancient Egypt were limestone, sandstone and granite. These were quarried from the hills above the Nile and taken to the building site by sledge or barge. Builders used saws and chisels made from metal and wood, and wooden mallets. Egyptian saws were among the earliest in the world. You can still see ancient saw marks on some of the pyramid stones.

► *The ruins of Deir el Medinah can still be seen today on the west bank of the River Nile.*

### IMPACT

Obelisks were tall, pointed stone columns, carved with dedications to the gods and kings. They were often put up in pairs. Cleopatra's Needle, which stands on the bank of the River Thames in London dates from the reign of Tuthmosis III (1479-1425 BC). Its pair stands in Central Park, New York. Other ancient obelisks can be seen in Paris, Rome and Istanbul.

*Cleopatra's Needle in London.*

## Tomb-builders

In an effort to protect them from robbers, the tombs of the New Kingdom pharaohs were cut deep into the rocks in the Valley of the Kings at Thebes. A permanent workforce of tomb-builders lived in the nearby village of Deir el Medinah. At its height, the village had some 120 houses. Today, only the stone foundations remain, but thousands of bills, receipts and letters have been found written on scraps of pottery and papyrus. These are a precious source of information about the builders' lives.

## At home

Tombs and temples were made from stone because they were built to last. But ordinary houses were made of mud bricks, hardened and dried in the sun. Poor people lived in small, cramped houses. It was often cooler and more comfortable to sleep on the flat roof. Wealthy people had large homes, in town or on their country estates.

▼ *A model of an Egyptian mud house. Models like this were often buried in people's tombs.*

# GODS AND TEMPLES

The Ancient Egyptians worshipped hundreds of gods and goddesses. Some were believed to control the forces of nature, such as the sun, the moon and the weather. Others were linked to aspects of daily life, such as farming or writing. Beautiful temples were built in honour of the gods, such as the temple of Amun-Re at Karnak, or dedicated to a dead king or queen. A statue of the god or king stood inside the temple. Some of these temples still stand today.

▼ The great hypostyle (columned) hall in the Temple of Amun-Re at Karnak.

## Reeds and flowers

Egyptian temples were built to mimic nature. The pillars in the hypostyle (columned) hall were carved to look like bundles of reeds. The tops of the columns were shaped like lotus blossoms. The lotus was a sacred flower, symbolizing the way the universe unfolded when it was created. The temples were painted with brilliant colours. They must have been a breathtaking sight.

▲ Pillars decorated with lotus flowers from the temple of Amun-Re.

## Priests and worship

Temples were believed to be the gods' homes on earth. They were private places, reserved for the gods and the priests and priestesses who served them. Ordinary people could only go as far as the entrance to leave offerings and pray. Most worshipped the gods at home. Every day, the priests made offerings to the god, dressed his statue and gave it food, as if it were alive.

▶ A statue of a priest of the goddess Hathor. She was the mother goddess of the pharaohs.

## Temple to the sun

Some gods were worshipped all over Egypt. During the New Kingdom, the most important god was Amun-Re, the sun god. His temple at Karnak was the largest in Egypt. The Great Hall alone had 134 columns, each more than 25 metres high. The columns and walls were carved with scenes showing the king worshipping Amun-Re. You can still visit the ruins of this great temple, which is the largest religious building ever constructed.

Two of the statues guarding the entrance to Ramesses' temple.

# FAMOUS PHARAOHS

The king was the most important person in Ancient Egypt. He was the absolute ruler of the country and his word was law. He was believed to be descended from the sun god, and to be the god Horus in human form. This gave him great power and authority. He was so holy that it was rude to call him by name. Instead he was called Pharaoh, from the Egyptian words per-o or great house, meaning the palace where he lived. Since then, the names of the pharaohs have been kept alive by the magnificent tombs and monuments raised in their honour.

## FAMOUS PEOPLE

Tutankhamun's tomb was discovered by British archaeologist, Howard Carter (1873-1939) after a search lasting almost 20 years. His patron, Lord Carnarvon, was present when the tomb was opened, but did not live to see the face of the king. He died six months later, struck down, rumour said, by the pharaoh's curse.

*Howard Carter inside Tutankhamun's tomb.*

◄ *Queen Hatshepsut wearing the royal headdress and beard!*

22

## King or queen?

The throne was usually passed down to the eldest son of the pharaoh's chief wife. Very few women became rulers. Perhaps the most extraordinary was Queen Hatshepsut (ruled 1473-1458 BC). At first, she acted as regent for her stepson, but later she was crowned king. She was addressed as 'His Majesty' and wore the pharaoh's crown and the ceremonial royal beard!

## How Egypt was governed

The king was the head of the government, but he left the day-to-day running of the country to his officials. The most important officials were the two viziers. One was in charge of Lower Egypt; the other of Upper Egypt. They acted as mayors, judges and tax collectors for the king. Each had a staff of officials, scribes and messengers who looked after the great state departments of the Treasury, Royal Works, Granaries and Foreign Affairs.

◄ *Ramesses II dressed for war. The king was commander-in-chief of the army.*

*The exquisite gold death mask of King Tutankhamun.*

## Warrior and builder

One of the most famous pharaohs of Ancient Egypt was Ramesses II. He ruled for 67 years from 1290-1224 BC. A great warrior, he brilliantly defeated the Hittites at the Battle of Kadesh in 1284 BC. He also built more temples and monuments than any other pharaoh. These included two of Egypt's most spectacular temples – Abu Simbel and the temple of Amun-Re at Karnak (see page 20).

# WRITING AND PAINTING

Writing began about 5500 years ago in Sumeria (modern Iraq). Shortly afterwards, the Egyptians developed a system of writing of their own. It used picture symbols, called hieroglyphs, to stand for objects and sounds. It meant that the Egyptians could write down their history, ideas and keep accurate records, rather than having to rely on memory. This was a very important landmark for Egyptian civilization, and for us today.

## IMPACT

The paintings found in Egyptian tombs tell us a great deal about everyday life. They show pleasant scenes of the Egyptians at home, at play and at work. They also show scenes from the life of the dead person, and from the lives of the gods and kings. But they were not simply painted for decoration. The Egyptians believed that in the next world the paintings would come to life so that the dead person could take part in them.

*Admiring the paintings inside an Ancient Egyptian tomb.*

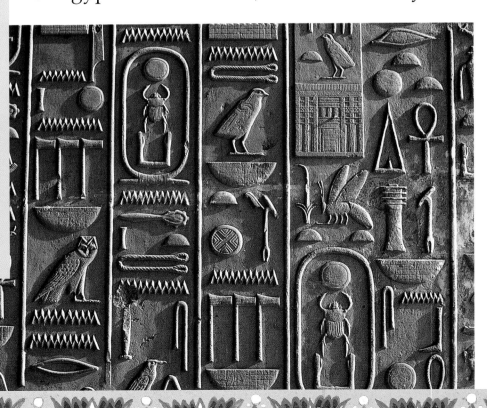

► *These Egyptian hieroglyphs spell out a dedication to the gods.*

## Scribes at work

Hieroglyphs were very complicated to use. Specially trained writers, called scribes, spent years learning to read and write them. Because their writing skills were so highly valued, many scribes rose to positions of power and status. Hieroglyphs were only used for affairs of state and inscriptions on temples and tombs. In everyday life, a simpler, shorthand style was used.

▶ Being a scribe was a well paid and well respected job in Ancient Egypt.

## FAMOUS PEOPLE

Until AD 1822, hieroglyphs remained a mystery. No one could read or understand them. Then a brilliant French scholar, Jean-François Champollion (1790-1832), managed to decipher the hieroglyphs on a large stone slab found near Rosetta in Egypt. The same text was written in hieroglyphs and Greek. By comparing the two, Champollion was finally able to crack the code.

The Rosetta Stone.

## Writing materials

The Ancient Egyptians had no paper or pens. They wrote on a paper-like material called papyrus, made from the reeds that grew along the river. This is where the word paper comes from. The inner stems were cut into strips, then arranged in overlapping layers. They were covered with cloth, then pounded with heavy stones or a mallet. Then the sheets were pasted together to form a long scroll. Instead of pens, scribes used hollow reeds, dipped into ink made of soot and water.

## Egyptian artists

Egyptian artists mainly used their skills to decorate tombs and temples. First the wall was covered in plaster, then a grid was marked out with string. This helped the artist to get his drawings in proportion. The outline of the picture was sketched in red, then the colour and details filled in. Perspective was not used realistically. Figures were usually shown in profile.

# WEIGHTS AND MEASURES

The Ancient Egyptians were expert mathematicians, engineers and scientists, with highly advanced systems of numbers and measuring. They were also practical people, putting their knowledge to good use in building and surveying. Some of their inventions were useful only in Egypt. These included gauges called nilometers, used to check the depth of the River Nile. Others had a lasting influence on later civilizations.

## FAMOUS PEOPLE

In 1858, Alexander Rhind (1833-1863), a Scottish collector of antiquities, made an amazing find. While on holiday in Luxor, he bought an ancient papyrus scroll. Written in about 1650 BC by a scribe called Ahmes, the Rhind Papyrus has become our main source of information about Egyptian mathematics. The papyrus is now in the British Museum, London.

*Part of the Rhind Papyrus.*

► *Nilometers were marks on rocks that showed the level of each year's flood.*

▲ *Surveyors measuring the wheat crop before it is harvested to work out the king's share.*

## Practical mathematics

The Ancient Egyptians used maths in many practical ways. Geometry was used to re-mark field boundaries when the annual flood washed them away. Accurate calculations were vitally important in the design of the pyramids. The base of the Great Pyramid was marked out in a square, with the angles at the corners equal to within a fraction of a degree.

## The royal cubit

The Egyptians based their units of measurement on the human body. They measured length in cubits, the length of a man's arm from his elbow to his middle fingertip. All cubit sticks were measured against the Royal Cubit, a black granite rod about 52 centimetres long. This prevented any confusion.

### IMPACT

Egyptian astronomers used the stars to work out one of the earliest calendars, some 5000 years ago. It was the first to divide the year into 365 days. The calendar began with the appearance of Sirius, the dog star, in the east, in the middle of June. This marked the start of the annual flood. The calendar we use today is called the Gregorian calendar. It is based on an earlier calendar devised by the Roman ruler, Julius Caesar. He, in turn, based his calendar on that of Ancient Egypt.

▲ *The oldest surviving water clock was found in the temple of Amun-Re in Karnak in 1905. It dates from the early fourteenth century BC.*

## Telling the time

The earliest known clocks were shadow clocks, invented in Ancient Egypt 4000 years ago. Water clocks were used from about 1500 BC. A water clock was a stone bucket with a hole in the bottom and a scale on the inside to mark the time as the water level fell. Water clocks became the standard way of telling the time in the ancient world. They remained in use until the thirteenth century.

# EGYPTIAN LIFE

O ur knowledge of everyday life in Ancient Egypt comes largely from the paintings and personal objects found in tombs. These have helped experts to build up a picture of what type of clothes the Egyptians wore, what food they ate, what sort of work they did and how they spent their leisure time.

## FAMOUS PEOPLE

Sometime during the Old Kingdom, a vizier called Ptahhotep, wrote a famous work in the form of a father giving advice to his son. It set out the values by which the Egyptians should live. For example, if you were invited to dinner by someone more important than you, you should eat whatever you were given, try not to stare and speak only when you were spoken to.

► *The beautiful Queen Nefertiti, wife of Akhenaten. She wears a necklace and headdress, eye make-up and lipstick.*

▲ *These Egyptian women are wearing incense cones on their heads, which gave out a sweet-smelling perfume.*

## Looking good

The Ancient Egyptians wore kilts, dresses and robes made of white linen. On their feet, they wore reed sandals. Personal appearance was very important. Wealthy Egyptians wore elaborate headdresses and wigs, even when they had perfectly good hair of their own. Both men and women liked wearing make-up. They coloured their lips and cheeks with red ochre (clay) and painted their eyes with black or green eyeliner. Henna was used as a hair dye, as it is today.

## Egyptian jewels

Everyone in Egypt loved wearing jewellery, especially necklaces, bracelets and rings. Jewellery-makers were highly skilled and created exquisite designs from gold and semi-precious stones, such as turquoise, garnet and amethyst. Their speciality was to decorate objects with gold beads. They also made jewellery boxes from ivory, wood and gold.

◄ *The exquisite scarab pectoral from Tutankhamun's tomb. It is made of gold inlaid with lapis lazuli and amber.*

## Playing games

Egyptian children played with toys such as rattles, dolls, balls, spinning tops and wooden animals. They also kept cats, dogs, birds and monkeys as pets. A board game called senet was extremely popular. It was played with a dice and counters, a bit like ludo or backgammon. Four senet boards were buried in Tutankhamun's tomb to keep him entertained.

▲ *One of the senet boards from Tutankhamun's tomb.*

### IMPACT

Ancient Egyptian doctors and surgeons were highly regarded throughout the ancient world. They were the first to study the body scientifically. They understood how to set broken bones using splints and casts, and had knowledge of the brain and heart. They wrote about their discoveries in specialist medical textbooks. Copies of parts of these amazing books still survive today.

29

# GLOSSARY

**absolute ruler** A ruler who rules by himself or herself and is the most powerful person in the country or state.

**antiquities** Objects and artefacts from ancient times.

**archaeologist** A person who studies human history by excavating and examining ruins and remains, such as ancient cities, burial sites and artefacts, such as pots and tools.

**Art Deco** A style of art that was very popular in the 1920s/30s. It borrowed patterns and styles used by the Ancient Egyptians.

**artefacts** Objects from ancient times, such as pots, tools, clothes and jewellery.

**backgammon** A game played on a board with counters and dice.

**capstone** The topmost stone on a building or pillar.

**civil war** A war fought between two groups of people from the same city or country.

**climate** The usual type of weather a place has over a long period of time. Ancient Egypt has a hot, dry climate.

**culture** A country or people's achievements in the arts, sciences and technology.

**decipher** To decode or make out the meaning of something, usually writing or numbers.

**decline** To become weaker or to come to an end.

**dedicate** To devote something like a building or a work of art to a god, a ruler or a friend.

**delta** The pattern of islands and channels at a river's mouth where the river flows into the sea. The islands are made up of mud and sand laid down by the river.

**dynasty** A ruling family where power is passed down from one member of the family to another.

**Egyptologists** Experts who study the life and culture of Ancient Egypt.

**empire** A large and powerful state, often made up of several countries and territories. It is ruled over by a single leader called an emperor or an empress.

**flax** A plant whose fibres are used to make a material called linen. The Ancient Egyptians made their clothes out of linen.

**granary** A building in which grain, such as wheat or corn, is stored.

**granite** A hard type of rock used for building.

**henna** An orange-red plant dye used in Ancient Egypt as a hair colour. It is still used today.

**hydroelectric power** Electricity produced by the force of running water from a river or lake.

**incense** A sweet-smelling mixture of spices often burned during religious ceremonies.

**inlaid** An object which is decorated with precious stones which are set slightly into its surface.

**inscription** A piece of writing on stone, metal or paper. Inscriptions often show the name of the person to whom an object or building is dedicated.

**irrigation** A system of canals, pipes and ditches that farmers use to bring water to their fields so that their crops can grow.

**lapis lazuli** A bright blue semi-precious stone. The Ancient Egyptians often used lapis lazuli to make jewellery.

**limestone** A type of stone that the Ancient Egyptians used for building their pyramids.

**mallet** A large wooden hammer.

**manoeuvrable** Easy to operate, move or steer.

**mimic** To copy something or someone.

**monarch** A ruler, such as a king, queen, emperor or empress who rules a country or state. He or she may rule alone or with a government.

**mortuary temple** A small temple that formed part of a pyramid complex. The king's body was taken there before being placed inside the pyramid.

**natron** A type of salt packed around a dead person's body to dry it out as part of the process of mummification.

**perspective** A way of painting or showing people and objects so that they appear to be bigger or smaller depending on how far they are apart. This is how they would look in real life. The Ancient Egyptians did not use perspective realistically.

**province** Roman territories outside Italy were called provinces. They were ruled on behalf of the Roman emperor by an official called a governor.

**regent** A person appointed to rule a country until the rightful king or queen is old enough to rule, or while the ruler is away.

**sandstone** A pinkish-orange stone used in building.

**scarab pectoral** A pendant in the shape of a scarab beetle which was worn around the neck. It was found in Tutankhamun's tomb.

**scholarship** Another name for study and learning.

**settlements** Villages, towns and cities where people live.

**status** A person's place or position in society, high or low.

**surveyor** A person who chooses and inspects a suitable site for a building. In Ancient Egypt, surveyors also measured out the boundaries of farmers' fields.

**symbolize** To stand for or signal something else. For example, the crown worn by a king or queen is a symbol of royal power.

**temple** In Ancient Egypt, a temple was a building dedicated to a god or goddess. It was thought to be the god's home on Earth.

# INDEX